super

# IN-LINE SKATING

## Philippa Perry

*Illustrated by Rowan Clifford*

Consultant: Anton Hilton,
Road Runner Skate Shop

*Hodder
Children's
Books*

a division of Hodder Headline

*The author would like to thank her friend Cake and all the crew at Road Runner Skate Shop. A special thank you to Stevie G who first said, "You've got to try this new craze from America."*

Text copyright 1999 © Philippa Perry
Illustrations copyright 1999 © Rowan Clifford
This edition published by Hodder Children's Books 2000

Series design by Fiona Webb
Book design by Joy Mutter
Project editor: Lyn Coutts
Consultant: Anton Hilton, Roadrunner Skate Shop, London

The right of Philippa Perry and Rowan Clifford to be identified as the author and illustrator of the work has been asserted by them in accordance with the Copyright, Designs and Patents Act 1988.

10 9 8 7 6 5 4 3 2 1

A catalogue record for this book is available from the British Library.

ISBN: 0 340 79152 7

Printed by Clays Ltd, St Ives plc.

Hodder Children's Books
a division of Hodder Headline
338 Euston Road
London NW1 3BH

# Meet the author

Philippa Perry is a freelance writer and author who has written many books for children. You may recognise her name from magazines like *Young Telegraph* or from her books *Olympic Gold*, *Mega Machines* and *Spooky Stories*. She's also written books about the police and the fire brigade for a series about teamwork.

She took up in-line skating in 1994 when there were just a handful of other bladers in London. She fell over a lot and has lots of scars (which she's quite proud of, actually) to prove it. She likes doing challenging things, which explains why Philippa is also into wing-walking and bungee jumping! When the weather's good you'll find her surfing, and when it's not she'll be snowboarding.

# Introduction

Go to any city in the world and you'll probably find kids and adults grinding rails, riding stairs, doing jumps, skating to work, exercising and doing amazing take-your-breath-away tricks on vert ramps. You may come also across hockey players on wheels and speed skaters that flash by you in a blur. All these guys have one thing in common: they're all in-line skaters.

But how do you get to be an ace in-line skater? How do you swizzle when you can't stand up? How do you ride with style? How do you find your local skate park? And how do you know which style of in-line skating is for you? To find out and to have more fun than you've ever dreamed, read on and enjoy the ride.

*Philippa Perry*

# Contents

# 1 Roll on ...

wow!

## The dream

It's rush hour in the skate park. The scene's really dope. There are no spores choking up the ramp where you're hangin' with your main crew. You catch some rays, then it's onto the vert ramp to get some air. Over to session the slalom, where you skate through 30 cones. A real crowd's beginning to build. Onto the street, avoiding road rash – you haven't slammed for weeks – you royale a 10-step rail, and session some planters and kerbs.

If you really want to in-line skate, then that could be your dream. And it's not impossible. In a matter of months, you could be sessioning a skate park like a real pro skater, playing roller hockey with your local team or winning speed skating competitions. All you need is the right attitude, a bit of skill and a lot of practice. But just how did this madness called in-line skating start?

## Get the lingo

*In-line skating, like skateboarding and snowboarding, has its own language. If you don't understand a word or term, look it up in the Glossary on pages 119-120.*

# First rollers

People have been skating since our early ancestors first attached animal bones or antlers to their boots to travel across frozen lakes. But it took an innovative Dutchman in the 1700s to come up with an idea for the first in-line skate. He was such a skate-addict, that he wouldn't take his ice skates off – even in the summer – so he nailed some wooden sewing-thread spools to the bottom of his skate boots and, hey presto, the first all-weather skate was born.

3

## Party crasher

In-line skating has always attracted individuals who like to stand out from the crowd. One of the first skating crazies was Joseph Merlin who decided to make a dramatic entrance to a fancy dress party in 1760. Merlin's skates consisted of a pair of walking boots attached to planks of wood. Fixed to the bottom of both planks

were four metal wheels. He cruised into the ballroom in a blaze of glory, but because he couldn't steer or stop, he ended up crashing into a huge mirror. It took a while to develop the perfect in-line skates and you can bet that a lot of other things were broken in the search for the ultimate wheel ride. But with each bruise, bash, graze and twisted ankle, came radical design and safety improvements.

### Blade runner

*In-line skating is often called rollerblading or simply blading. The term "blade" comes from the company, Rollerblade, that was founded by in-line skating innovator, Scott Olsen.*

By the 1860s inventors realised that the boots needed to be high and reasonably solid to protect the ankle, and that more wheels allowed greater flexibility and speed. The invention of ball bearing wheels in 1884 was a big leap forward in the history of the sport. Ball-bearings made it possible for skaters to perform tight turns, mean tricks and backward moves.

*Check out the wheels, man!*

## High rider – Matt Salerno

*Matt is a Down-under, professional vert and street skater from Sydney who became totalled on the sport when he went to see a half-pipe demonstration. He tries to achieve a personal best every time he hits the ramp. When not in-lining, Matt can be found in the pipeline – not the half-pipe – on his surfboard.*

## Flashing blades

In-lining took a massive jump forward in the early 1980s when an American called Scott Olsen, found an old in-line skate when rummaging around in the back of a sport shop. He was a top ice-hockey player and immediately realised how useful in-line skates would be for out-of-season training off the ice.

Scott added a heel brake to a four-wheeled, high-sided hockey-style boot. With his brand new boot, Olsen also founded Rollerblade Inc – one of the biggest manufacturers of in-line equipment in the world.

## Born in the USA

In-lining really took off in the United States in the 1980s. Once the equipment had been perfected, there was no stopping the sport. There was huge interest from hockey skaters, cross-country skiers and people just wanting to get fit. People skated anywhere and everywhere they could find a smooth ride – along the beach front, through the parks and on the streets.

In many places, especially the big cities such as Los Angeles, in-line skating became almost as popular as jogging as a way of keeping fit. But more than that, it was a seen as a cool mode of transport. With a back-pack strapped to their back, shades to cut the glare and a lid on their head, LA in-liners could go anywhere.

Central Park in New York is one of the best places to skate in the world. As well as the wide open outer carriage-way, free from cars and buses where you can speed skate, there are special areas for freestyle jumping, dancing, ramps, slalom courses and figure skating, as well as heaps of steps, rails and curbs for aggressive skaters to ride. Skate heaven!

## Burning rubber, burning energy

*In-line skating will burn up lots of energy – about 570 calories an hour – so don't hit the park or ramp on an empty stomach. Pack some nutritious snacks (fruit, sandwiches, museli bars) in your back-pack along with a plastic container of water – in-lining is thirsty work!*

## Roll on ...

Wherever they went, Americans took their sport with them. Soon the word spread and people everywhere were taking up in-line skating. By the early 1990's, in-line skating was big, big business, popular from Tasmania to Tokyo, Mexico to Manchester. In-line skating was here to stay.

## Types of in-line skating

Today it's a sport with several different branches – recreational, aggressive, roller hockey and speed skating, and each encourage new talent with tournaments, championships, competitions and leagues.

### AGGRESSIVE SKATING
There are two types – street skating and vertical skating. Street skaters use the street as their playground, performing tricks and jumps on objects they find around them, such as stairs, rails, curbs and benches. Vertical skaters perform their moves on specially-designed vert ramps.

### IN-LINE HOCKEY
Very much like ice hockey, but without the ice. Requires great stamina, ace skate skills and teamwork.

### SPEED SKATING
Short- or long-distance races on in-line skates. Crossing the line first, setting the fastest time and beating their own best time is the aim of all competitors.

8

# Get in line

You don't need to be gifted, highly co-ordinated or particularly fit to skate, though it does help. People of all ages, shapes and sizes can learn.

Before you can hit the hard stuff, you'll need to get geared up, and that means – as well as skates – getting hold of protective pads and a helmet. Don't even contemplate going out without the protective stuff – you'll end up as bashed as a banana in a bag of nails.

## In-line for the Olympics

*In 1996, in-line speed skating was an exhibition sport at the Atlanta Olympics. Move over, synchronised swimming!*

# Pad up!

*Most or all skating takes place on concrete, asphalt, brick, wood or rubber. If you hit the deck on this stuff even the rubberised surfaces – you're going to get road rash (broken skin or bones) or some nasty bruises.*

*The way to avoid road rash is to wear protective gear. There is some form of padding or similar that will protect every part of your body. Protective gear is designed extremely well and it works. It will let you improve your technique and give you the confidence to try new moves without being afraid of the occasional – but inevitable – tumble.*

*"Ok," you say, "but some skaters wear no protective gear at all. How come?"*

*Well, some skaters just don't think and others, most probably highly-experienced skaters, are willing to take a calculated risk that they are skating well within their capabilities and that a fall is unlikely. But even pros will don protective gear when training for a competition (they don't want to be carrying an injury that could harm their chances of winning or competing) or when trying new moves.*

## WRIST GUARDS

*Plastic splints inside wrist guards prevent you from straining or breaking your wrists if you break a fall with your hands. If you wear no other protective gear, say the pros, wear these.*

## ELBOW PADS

*Protect elbows with these pads that fasten with Velcro straps above and below the elbow. Essential for beginners.*

## KNEE PADS

*The best kind have wrap-around padding that protects the front and sides of the knees. Make sure they fasten securely. Even if you're moving slowly, an encounter with the pavement can cause cuts and bruises. And let's face it, bruises are not the coolest-looking things in the world. Essential for aggressive and hockey skating.*

## HELMET (OR LID)

*The main reason for wearing a helmet is to protect your head, but it also has the added advantage of making you standout in people traffic. Look out for the newer designs that offer special protection to the back of the head. Check that your helmet meets required government regulations. Some skate parks insist that helmets are worn.*

## BAGGY TROUSERS OR LONG SHORTS

*You can wear what you like when you in-line, although each type of skating has developed its own look. Loose-fitting, heavy-duty, cool threads are best for aggressive skaters, while speed skaters wear tight-fitting clothes.*

## SWEATSHIRT, LONG-SLEEVE SHIRTS OR T-SHIRTS

*You don't need labels to in-line or lots of branded gear. Real pros just wear what feels right.*

*And last but not least, you need ...*

## IN-LINE SKATES

*Whatever type of in-line skating you get in to, it's important that you have good skates. A dodgy pair could cause a nasty fall and make it hard for you to develop your talent. There's more about choosing skates on pages 15-26.*

# Dressed in line

Skate clothing needs to be able to take a beating but still look good. It's also important that the clothes allow you to move freely. Your skating style goes down the gurgler if you're trussed up like an Egyptian mummy.

*Helmet* – adjust the strap and padding to get a snug fit. If the helmet wobbles around on your head, it's not going to do its job.

*Long sleeve shirt or sweatshirt* – look good and offer a bit of protection for your arms.

*T-shirt* – baggy is best.

*Elbow pads* – you know there's nothing to laugh about when you hit your funny bone!

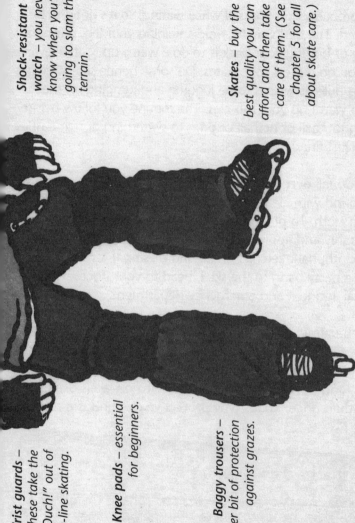

**Shock-resistant watch** – you never know when you're going to slam the terrain.

**Skates** – buy the best quality you can afford and then take care of them. (See chapter 5 for all about skate care.)

**Wrist guards** – these take the "Ouch!" out of in-line skating.

**Knee pads** – essential for beginners.

**Baggy trousers** – another bit of protection against grazes.

# Gain not pain

You'll probably hurt yourself while skating, so it's good to be prepared. The best way to avoid spraining your leg, pulling a muscle or hurting your back is to do a warm-up routine every time you go out on your skates. Do some gentle side stretches and leg pulls as well as some jogging and jumping on the spot to warm up your muscles. The routine you follow before playing football or netball or prior to swimming or gymnastics will do just fine.

If you do fall over and graze yourself, remember to wash the wound with clean water (mineral water is perfect) and a clean cloth. To protect the wound until you wash it more thoroughly and apply a cream or dressing, cover it with a clean cloth, handkerchief or sticking plaster. If it's a deep cut or a nasty bang to the skull, head to your doctor or to a hospital accident and emergency department.

Don't be afraid of falling, it's part of the learning curve. All the best skaters spend hours on their backsides conquering new moves. Aggressive skaters will have probably hit their heads, and bashed their knees and shins on walls or railings more than once. That's why protective clothing is a must!

## High rider – Fab Fabiola

*Eighteen-year-old Fabiola is the top-ranked female vert skater in the world. She is one of the few women in aggressive skating and a great representative of cutting-edge fashion. Fabiola always piles on the protective gear when skating.*

## Skating on iron wheels

*Early skates were really uncomfortable. They had just two iron wheels (image the ride!) and leather straps that buckled around the ankle and over the foot. Women's skates were even more diabolical. They had a high heel (fashion victims, or what?) with a wheel underneath. If this was not enough torture, these ancient ancestors of today's refined skate had no brake. And your parents think that modern in-line skating is a dangerous sport!*

# Wheely good ideas

So you're ready to buy your first pair of skates. Well, take a deep breath because choosing your skates is a daunting, mind-boggling task.

As well as the wide selection of brands on offer, you've first got to decide what kind of skating is your bag. Do you want to perform tricks to make your granny faint and your mates green with envy? Do you want to skate to keep fit? Is skating just a fun way of doing a paper-round in an enviro-friendly manner? Is roller hockey or speed skating your idea of a good day out?

There are four different types of skates, each specially adapted for the kind of skating you want to do: recreational, aggressive, speed and hockey.

Most people tend to start off with recreational skates. These are great to learn on and no end of fun. Once you've developed some skills, you can then decide to specialise. You don't have to specialise, of course. If you and recreational skating are a bonded thing, then why change?

# Recreational skates

This is the basic recreational skate. It's perfect for beginners and intermediate skaters, or if you want to use your skates as a means of getting around. Rec skates are flexible and comfortable and therefore fine for long skating sessions. The heel brake is quite big (aggressive skaters discard the brake completely) and it needs to be if you're street-skating and trying to avoid pedestrians, dogs and kids on tricycles. There are lots of different makes of rec skates in the shops, but try to buy the best you can afford.

*Heel brake – can be square or round. You can buy recreational skates without a brake. The brake is removable and replaceable.*

*Bearings – hidden inside each wheel, these guarantee smooth-running wheels and therefore a smoother ride. High-precision bearings will allow the wheels to rotate faster.*

*Frame or chassis*

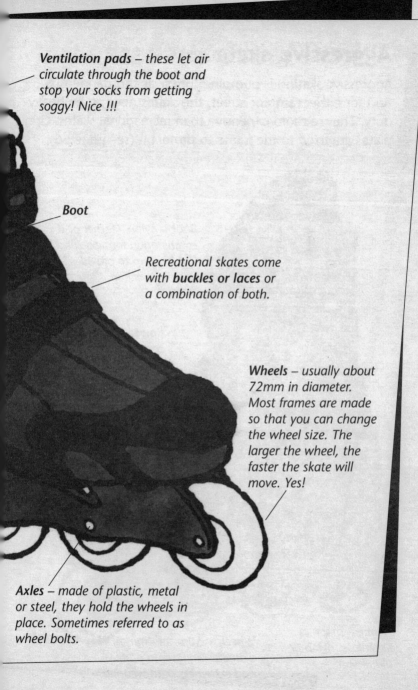

**Ventilation pads** – these let air circulate through the boot and stop your socks from getting soggy! Nice !!!

**Boot**

Recreational skates come with **buckles or laces** or a combination of both.

**Wheels** – usually about 72mm in diameter. Most frames are made so that you can change the wheel size. The larger the wheel, the faster the skate will move. Yes!

**Axles** – made of plastic, metal or steel, they hold the wheels in place. Sometimes referred to as wheel bolts.

# Aggressive skate

Aggressive skating is pumping, physical and dangerous. And for either ramp or street, the skates need to be heavy-duty. They're more expensive than recreational skates. Grind plates are fixed to the frame to protect it (see page 66).

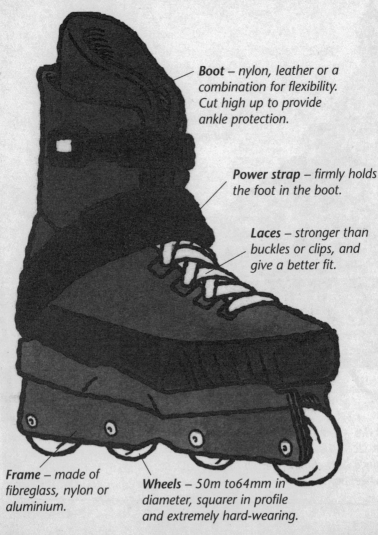

*Boot* – nylon, leather or a combination for flexibility. Cut high up to provide ankle protection.

*Power strap* – firmly holds the foot in the boot.

*Laces* – stronger than buckles or clips, and give a better fit.

*Frame* – made of fibreglass, nylon or aluminium.

*Wheels* – 50m to64mm in diameter, squarer in profile and extremely hard-wearing.

# /Speed skate

If you feel the need for speed, then speed skating could be the in-line sport for you. It's very fast and very exciting, but you need to be super fit. The only problem is that if you go all the way with this sport, you could end up looking like a blur in a tight plastic bag.

Speed skates are very expensive. A bottom-of-the-range pair of racing skates will set you back the equivalent of 40 CDs. Gulp!

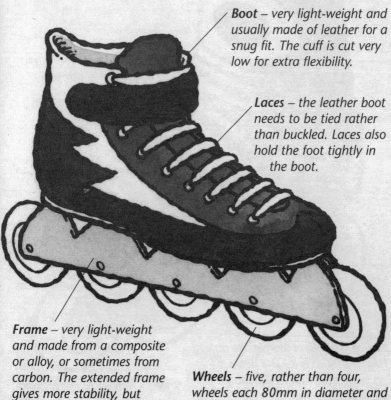

**Boot** – *very light-weight and usually made of leather for a snug fit. The cuff is cut very low for extra flexibility.*

**Laces** – *the leather boot needs to be tied rather than buckled. Laces also hold the foot tightly in the boot.*

**Frame** – *very light-weight and made from a composite or alloy, or sometimes from carbon. The extended frame gives more stability, but makes tight turns tough.*

**Wheels** – *five, rather than four, wheels each 80mm in diameter and very hard so that you can roll faster and do it for longer.*

# Hockey skate

Ever played roller hockey? If not, why not? It's one of the greatest sports going. Aside from the thrill of playing, you'll get to make friends, form a team and maybe even enter a league. It's a fat laugh.

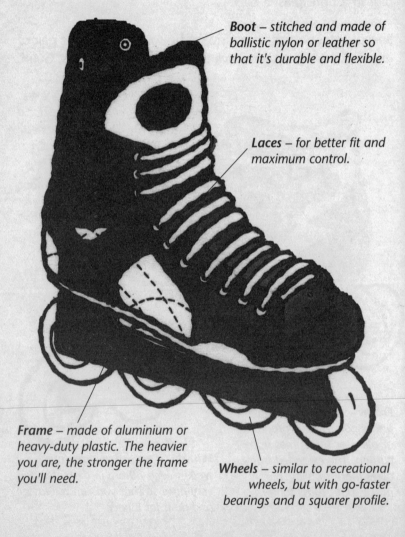

**Boot** – *stitched and made of ballistic nylon or leather so that it's durable and flexible.*

**Laces** – *for better fit and maximum control.*

**Frame** – *made of aluminium or heavy-duty plastic. The heavier you are, the stronger the frame you'll need.*

**Wheels** – *similar to recreational wheels, but with go-faster bearings and a squarer profile.*

20

# Putting the boot in

You've decided which type of in-lining you want to try,
you've got the clothes, the shades and it's time to get in
gear. The complete kit could set you back a lot of money
so rather than breaking open the bank for a sport you've
just got a hankering for, it's a good time to rent first to see
if you really take to it.

There are lots of different shops who rent skates. You'll
usually find the best ones close to your local skate park.
Always choose a reputable shop, smaller is usually better,
where the sales people are skaters themselves. Look at the
equipment. If it's badly scuffed and bashed around you
may be better off trying somewhere else. Look for a skate
shop that sells magazines, videos, cool threads and for sales
assistants that are wearing skates. These guys are real fans!

# Top tips for buying skates

*So you've been out a few times on hire skates and pads, hit the deck a few times and now you're ready to trade in the hire skates for a pair of your own. Here's how to go about it and what to watch out for:*

**1** *Always buy from a specialist in-line shop that stocks lots of different makes of skates. Department stores are not good places to buy, despite their cheap prices. They may only stock one brand of skate and the sales staff may not be skaters themselves. Specialist shops have spare parts, hop up kits and you'll be able to go back to them for advice.*

**2** *Make sure the sales assistants are skaters themselves, they'll be able to give you the best advice about boots, bearings and wheels.*

**3** *Don't buy the coolest-looking pair of skates. It's much more important that the boots fit well and that they feel really comfortable.*

**4** *Always buy the protective gear – wrist guards, elbow and knee pads, and helmet – at the same time as you buy the skates.*

**5** *Buy your skates well before the summer season begins. You're bound to come across some good* bargains and the sales assistants will be able to devote a fair amount of time to getting you set up properly.

## Sales babble

Don't be fooled into buying skates or any other gear that you're not really happy with. If you're going to part with some serious money, then you may need this code to decipher sales babble:

**Sales-speak** – "These are the latest design and colour."

**Meaning** – "We've had these for eons and we just can't shift them."

**Sales-speak** – "You look great in those."

**Meaning** – "You're going to eat pavement."

**Sales-speak** – "Everyone'll be wearing these sweatshirts this winter."

**Meaning** – "If you buy this, I get a commission and a holiday in Barbados."

Don't be taken in by sales talk, it will cost more than you think!

Oooh!
Suits you
Sir, suits you

23

# The family of skates

There are lots of different makes of skates to choose from including K2's, Roces, Rollerblades, Bauer, Oxygen and In-liners to name a few. There are skates for girls and skates for boys; detachable skates; rainbow-coloured skates; skates with straps; and skates with buckles, tongues and grooves. And with names like Tribe, Rebel, Lightning and Nitroblade, some skates sound more like the cast list of an episode of *Gladiators* than boots!

Skate manufacturers, just like manufacturers of other sports equipment, are constantly competing with each other to make the ultimate skate. They sponsor professional skaters and produce add-ons, gadgets and trendy gear to make their brand more attractive than any other.

## Simply the best?

In reality, there's no one quality brand that is essentially better than the rest. The perfect skate is the one that suits your purpose, is extremely comfortable and matches your budget. The only way to find your Cinderella-skate is to try on as many as you can. And don't just slip them on and take a hesitate step, do up the buckles and laces and take them for a walk around the shop.

If you feel that you're getting nowhere, ask around. Fellow skaters will be only too happy to dish the dirt or sing the praises about certain skate brands or designs. They will also point you in the right direction for great skate shops. (To find out the latest on new skates, see pages 116-118).

One thing to remember: no skate will make you a better skater. Only practice, skill and determination can do that.

## What's it to be: buckles or laces?

So you've finally plumped for the make of skates you like, but do you go for laces or buckles, an integrated brake pad or a detachable one? Yup, it's really very confusing. Skate manufacturers are constantly bringing out new bits of equipment; it's amazing that anyone ever makes it out of the shop and onto the street. However, when it comes to buckles and laces, there are advantages and disadvantages:

### Buckles
**Pros**: Buckles tend to hold your foot more firmly; there's no loosening as you skate.
**Cons:** There's not so much give or flexibility.

### Laces
**Pros**: They provide a better fit and greater flexibility.
**Cons:** They're not quite as safe because your feet can move around inside the boot a bit too much.

As you can see there are advantages and disadvantages on both sides. The main thing is to find which works best for you. Some pros go for laces and some for buckles, and some opt for a combination of the two.

## To brake or not to brake?

As you get better and better, you should aim to learn stopping moves that will allow you to throw the brake away. But brakes are essential when you're just starting. Even when your confidence level and your skill are on an upward curve, don't chuck the brake away too quickly – you never know when you might need it.

The simple truth is that for most advanced and experienced skaters brakes are uncool. Check out the best skaters in the park; they don't use brakes, they slow down and stop using all kinds of different moves.

# Time to roll

So you've made it out of the shop. You've got the skates you've always dreamed about, all the gear and you look cooler than S.O. Cool, winner of the all-comers cool competition. It's a beautiful sunny day, perfect for learning to in-line, and you're finally ready to roll.

In this chapter, we'll look at safe places to learn to skate, how to glide, how to stop, how to make it at the skate park and let you in on some skate smart tips.

## Padded up and ready to launch

*Okay, so you're all padded up and feel like a) gridiron, footballer, b) Terminator and c) the Michelin Man. Well, if it's of any comfort you don't look like any of them. But you do look like a skater who's going to get down to some stunts, confident in the knowledge that slams may hurt your pride but not your knees, elbows, hands, head etc etc etc.*

# Where to skate?

The answer is basically any where you like as long as it's SAFE! Take risks now and you'll never get to try out the mean tricks in chapter 6.

The best way to find the places to skate is by asking other skaters or your nearest skate shop. Here are some suggestions: local parks, empty school playgrounds (get permission first), indoor and outdoor running tracks, bicycle paths, quiet pavements, seaside promenades (got to be the best) and, of course, skate parks. But until you've learned to control those things attached to your feet, street skating is a safety no-no.

## Skates a no-go

1 Don't skate where there is traffic.
2 Don't skate on gravel.
3 Don't skate on private property.
4 Take extra care when skating near water. One tiny slip and both you and your precious skates get very wet.
5 Don't skate at night on pavements or roads. At dusk, don reflective gear and keep your eyes and ears open.
6 Can't in-line without techno blasting your eardrums? Then stay well away from people, bike and vehicle traffic. You have been warned!!!

## Wheels away!

*Don't try your first moves on a hill or slope. Your wheels will roll away from under you. Oops!*

## Carpet skate

If you don't want to take your first shaky steps in your skates under the watchful gaze of your mates, why not try them out in the living room? The shag pile will prevent the skates from rolling out from under you, and if they do – which they won't – where better to land than on a soft, squishy sofa?

Your initial encounter in skate world is a bit strange. For a start you'll be about 10 centimetres taller, your feet may feel like they're set in concrete blocks and you may doubt whether you'll ever master skating let alone walking again. But relax, within no time at all you'll be skating in your sleep.

### Golden rules

**1** It's early days yet, so don't try skating to a local park or skate park. Ask a parent for a lift or walk there carrying your skates.

**2** The best paths are dead level (traversing slopes comes later), smooth (forget cobble- or flag-stoned paths littered with twigs) and reasonably wide. If the path has smooth run-offs on both sides to grass (in other words, no curbs or raised concrete edges), even better. You can use the grass to slow you down or to cushion a fall.

**3** In the early stages of learning it's not wise to try mixing it with people, dogs, kids, skateboarders, trees or cyclists. In other words, you should have the path to yourself.

**4** Check your skates each time you put them on. There's all about maintenance in chapter 5.

# First moves

### STEP 1

Keep your feet about 25 centimetres apart. Your knees should be slightly bent and you should try to keep your weight forward with your centre of gravity at your hips. Don't look at your feet as it will unbalance you. Keep your eyes on what's ahead. Remember to relax – this is meant to be fun!

### STEP 2

Raise your hands to about waist level. Do a series of movements where you shift your weight from one leg to the other. Push your toes slightly outwards. The V-shape will help you balance. Now, raise one skate off the ground and balance on the other skate for as long as you can. Repeat the exercise, this time raising the other skate.

## Losing your balance?

Always keep relaxed and loose.
If you are too stiff, the slightest
buckle or crack in the pavement
will make you fall over. If you
feel yourself slipping or
becoming unsteady, bring your
hands onto your knees to
steady yourself.

## Fall safe

If you do fall, always fall onto your knees first and then
stretch outwards, sliding safely onto your wrist guards and
elbow pads.

To get up from a kneeling position, place one skate on the
ground just in front of you and rest both
hands on the bent knee. Start to stand up,
keeping your weight on your hands.
Keep both knees bent until
you have regained
your balance.

# Stroke and glide

The stroke is what gets you and your skates moving. The glide helps you to roll faster.

### STEP 1
Starting with your feet in the V position, push your right skate out to the side and then return it to its starting position. Repeat this stroke move with your left skate.

### STEP 2
Shift your weight onto your right foot and glide. While the right glides, push off or stroke with the left foot. Congrats, you've done your first stroke and glide cycle.

## Pro talk

*"Watch the good skaters. They're the ones that keep their body totally relaxed."*
Matt Salerno, champion skater

### STEP 3

In between each stroke and glide, roll along with your feet parallel so that you can get your balance. This is called parallel rolling. Keep your weight on the balls of your feet and your arms out in front.

### STEP 4

Now do the same stroke/glide move but let the left foot do the glide while the right pushes. In between each stroke, roll along with your feet parallel so that you can get your balance.

## Pro talk

*"If you can glide on one leg for more than 30 seconds then you're well on your way."*
Charlie Cuthbertson, aggressive pro skater

# Stopping

Once you've got the basic stroke/glide going, the next thing to learn is how to slow down and stop. Being able to slow down and stop exactly when you want means that you'll have a lot more confidence and be able to get on much faster. You'll also be able to go down hills (very important), get out of trouble much more quickly and avoid out-of-control spores (extremely important).

There are lots of different ways of stopping, and it won't be long before you start inventing your own methods.

### RUNNING OUT

If you're going too fast, the easiest way to stop is to run onto grass. Point yourself away from the hard stuff and look for a soft landing.

When you're running out, keep your body position low and bend your knees to an angle of about 90 degrees. This will help you to keep your balance. Don't let your arms flail about. Keep them bent at the elbow and out in front of you.

### SOLID OBJECTS

To stop in an emergency or if you're simply out of control, point yourself towards a stationary object like a lamp post, wall or railing (people are NOT stationary objects!). Push against it with your outstretched hands. Use this method when you have no other choice and only use it when you're wearing protective padding and a helmet.

# Putting the brake on

It's important to learn how to slow down
and to stop using the brake, even if
you decide to discard it later. Your
first pair of skates should have a brake
on the right boot. If you're using second-hand
skates, check that the brake is firmly attached
and not worn (see also page 60).

## STEP 1  ▶

Move from a glide into a parallel roll with
your feet about 10 to 15 centimetres apart.
Make sure your knees are bent and your arms
are out in front of you.

## ◀ STEP 2

Move the right skate with the
brake forward so that the heel
of the braking skate is in line
with the toe of the left skate.
Keep your body low.

## STEP 3  ▶

Raise the toe of the right boot so that
the brake scrapes along the ground.
Use your arms to keep your balance.

35

### T-STOP

This is radical method of stopping quickly that is used by skaters who have discarded the brake.

Form a T-shape with one blade horizontally behind the other and flattened hard to the ground. Shift your weight onto you back foot and balance on the front foot. With the wheels dragging along the ground, you will stop quite quickly. The T-stop is not kind to wheels, so use it only when necessary.

## Look, one foot!

*Top in-liners are masters of speed control. They can decelerate by standing only on one foot.*

# Go slow

### MAKING TRIANGLES

A really cool-looking way to slow down is by forming a triangle shape with your knees and feet. Basically, this works by driving the knee of the trailing leg into the back of the knee of the leading leg. This provides stability and control. As you perfect this move, you'll be able to put more weight onto the leading foot.

## SLALOM

Keep your feet about 30 centimetres apart and move your hips to control your feet. This weight shift will make you cut a curvy path and therefore cut your speed. (For more about the slalom, see page 47.)

## SNOW PLOUGH

Make a V-shape by pointing the front of your boots inwards as shown. Very effective and very easy to do – ask a snow skier, they snow plough all the time!

## HOCKEY STOP

Also known as a powerslide, this cool but tricky stopping move is used by ice hockey players. It involves making a sharp, fast turn to the left and then to the right. Lean your body in to each turn and push your skates away from the centre of the turn. This forces your skates to slide across the surface.

# Skate smart

**Don't be a pavement hog.** Pedestrians and other park users have right of way. Let pedestrians know which way you are heading.

**Cut your speed around blind corners.** You don't know what's coming your way.

**Obey all signs in a public park** (especially the ones that say "No skating"!) and obey all normal traffic and road safety rules.

**Watch out for babies, children and dogs.** All of them are attracted to things on wheels and it's just impossible to predict what they're going to do!

**Never skate out of control in a busy park.** You'll hurt yourself and someone else.

**Don't skate in the rain.** Rain makes everything slippery and will cause wheel bearings to rust and seize up.

**Avoid sand, mud and puddles.** All these things can clog up your wheels and bearings.

**Don't skate when injured.**

# How's it rolling?

*How did you go on your first skate outing? Circle your answers, then check out your skate-rate.*

**1** *Did you fall over?* Yes No

**2** *Have you used the grass to stop yourself?*
Yes No

**3** *Have you been having a laugh?*
Yes No

**4** *Do your skates feel comfortable?*
Yes No

**5** *Have you asked other skaters for advice?*
Yes No

## YOUR SKATE-RATE

### Mostly Yes
*You're a natural in-line skater. Not even ending up on your backside fazes you. Way to go!*

### Mostly No
*You've got to gen-up on the technical stuff and get the right attitude. Relax and have a laugh – it's not a maths lesson after all. Don't be afraid to ask other skaters for advice, they'll be helpful and flattered.*

# 4 Getting on

The moves in this chapter will take you from novice to advanced beginner. Like all things worth doing, in-line skating requires practice and patience. If you can't get the hang of something, watch how other skaters do it.

Once you've mastered the moves in this chapter, it's time to ask yourself which area of the sport you're interested in – roller hockey, aggressive or speed. It will also be time to start developing an individual style and making up your own moves.

## High rider – Chris Garrett

*This guy tried them all – skateboarding, surfing and snowboarding – before hitting on in-line skating. This Californian's exhibition of vert skating dazzled the crowds at the 1996 Atlanta Olympics.*

# Warming up is cool

There are lots of fun exercises that will prepare you for more advanced skating. Some of these moves will become, or may have already become, part of your natural skating routine. The best thing about skating is that you can feel your way as you relax into the sport.

## In and out

This exercise, also known as a forward swizzle or sculling, is is great for building strength, improving balance and showing you how to use the inside edges of your skates.

### ◄ STEP 1

Stand with your knees bent, toes in the V position, and arms out in front of you. Bend your knees deeper and pushing into the ground with the inside edges of your skates. Lean forward all the time.

## STEP 2

Pushing should move your legs into a shoulder-width or wider position. Point your toes inward and bring your feet together again. ►

41

## Rocking

This exercise will prepare you for skating backwards. It consists of swizzling forwards and then backwards.

**STEP 1**

Do an in and out movement forward so your toes point inwards. Then push into the inside edges while putting more pressure on the balls of your feet. As you push your inside edges away from you, you'll begin to move backwards.

**STEP 2**

Keep your knees bent all the time and push into the ground with the balls of your feet. Roll backwards off your toes on the inside edges of your skates.

### Pro talk

*"Before you can get into aggressive skating, you have to learn the basics – all about balance, keeping a relaxed posture, moving forwards and backwards, turning, stopping and slowing."*

Charlie Cuthbertson, aggressive pro skater

# What a turn on

Doing great turns is one of the biggest buzzes. If you've ever been skiing or snowboarding, you'll know the exhilarating feeling of carving out long turns or quick small ones in the snow. Once you can turn on a Smartie, your skating pastures will suddenly be endless.

## TURNING TIPS

**1 Trust your edges**. The design of the wheels allows you to lean the skates over onto the edges without slipping.

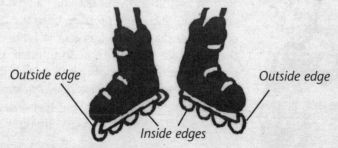

*Outside edge*                                    *Outside edge*

*Inside edges*

**2 Look where you're going.**
**3 Practise turning in both directions.** If you only feel comfortable making left turns, for example, you'll be going round in circles all day!

# A-frame turn

The A-frame turn is the first turn you need to learn. It's easy to do because your feet are spread apart to give you lots of stability. It's called an A-frame turn because your body makes an A-shape. Amazing, huh?

**◀ STEP 1**
Learn this turn on a smooth, level surface. Glide forwards in the A-shape posture with your feet spread a little wider than your hips. Place your weight evenly over both skates. Keep your head up and look where you're going. Your arms are out in front of you.

**STEP 2** ▲
To turn right, bend your left knee a little so you are putting more pressure onto the front of your left skate. Push out your left foot so that the skate starts to turn. To turn left, put extra pressure on the right skate so that it starts to turn. Your feet should always remain spread in the A-frame turn; your toes always pointing in the direction you're turning.

**◀ STEP 3**
Come out of the turn and go into a parallel roll (see page 33).

44

# Crossover turn

Crossover turns let you turn without losing any speed. Practise this turn on an open, level, hard-rolling surface.

## STEP 1 ▶

Do a few forward glides and moves, and then extend your right foot forward. Begin a coasting turn to the right by shifting your weight onto the right skate.

◀ ## STEP 2

Raise the left skate and cross it over the front of the right one. (This is the stepover.) Keep your right knee bent to help you balance. Place the left skate on the ground. The left skate will be rolling on the inside edge, the right skate on the outside.

## STEP 3

Return the right skate to the normal position. Try the same move with the left leg.

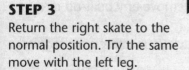

## Skating by numbers

*Practise cutting turning patterns like figures of eight or loopy threes. Slick turns are great to watch and even better to perform. If you want to see some fast crossover moves, watch ace ice skaters working a rink.*

# Keeping up appearances

Since you've probably shelled out quite a lot of money for your first pair of blades, you'll want to keep them looking and rolling as good as the day you bought them.

You can, of course, replace almost every bit on your skates. New wheels, brakes and bearings can be bought separately, and some skate shops will carry out the repair work and set up your skates for a small cost. But there are some really useful and dead-easy things you can do at home and on the road to keep your skates moving:

**1** Avoid riding through sand and mud, and don't take your skates out in the rain. These will all play havoc with the bearings. If the bearings are wearing, you'll hear a grinding sound when you spin the wheels. Not good!

**2** Wipe bearings with a clean, smooth cloth after you've been out for a heavy session to remove any built-up dirt.

**3** Keep the boots clean and check your safety gear regularly.

**4** Wheels wear down, so to get the most out of them you should rotate them regularly (see page 61).

# Cone head

Slalom – weaving in and out of a line of cones or other obstacles – is great fun, looks cool and and will help you perfect sharp turns and edging moves.

Create a slalom course on a slight slope with plastic cups or cones spaced one or two metres apart in a straight line. As you gain confidence, move the cones closer together.

### ◀ STEP 1

Skate towards the course at a comfortable speed, keeping your knees bent and holding a low-stance position. As you approach the first cone for a left-hand turn, your right foot takes a slight lead.

### STEP 2 ▶

When alongside the cone, swivel your hips and knees to the left. Work smoothly around the cone on the outside edge of the left skate and on the inside edge of the right. Once around the cone, move into parallel rolling and get ready for the next cone.

### ◀ STEP 3

To make the left-hand turn around the next cone, push the left skate into the lead. Swivel your hips and your knees to the left. Roll around the cone on the outside edge of the right skate and on the inside edge of the left.

# It's a revolution!

A 360-turn on the spot is nice trick that will earn you lots of cred. It's also a cool way to stop, which is why it's also known as a spin stop. The trick is to keep your balance as you spin in a tight circle. Always look in the direction you're going – your body and feet have the happy knack of following your head and eyes.

Once you've mastered turning one full circle, go for a 540-degree turn (that's about $1^1/_2$ revolutions) or even a 720-degree turn (that's two complete revolutions). Conquer a 720 and you'll no doubt hear your mates gasp in admiration.

## 360 turn

### STEP 1  ▶

To spin to the right, start from a ready position with your arms out in front for balance and your feet about 30 centimetres apart. Put your left skate, heel raised, in a trailing position. Keep the front wheel rolling smoothly along the ground.

### Snug turn

*If your ankles move too freely inside the boots, you won't be able to control a tight turn. Tighten the laces or adjust the buckles for a really snug fit.*

◀ **STEP 2**

Turn your left knee outwards by pivoting on the front wheel of the left skate. This will force your legs apart and the right skate will turn and glide. Ground the left skate so that all the wheels make contact. The heels of both skates should be close together with the toes splayed outwards. Your knees should be bent.

**STEP 3** ▶

If all has gone to plan, you should be spinning. Use your arms to keep you balanced and look in the direction of the spin. Don't worry if your first 360 is more than ride around the block than a spin on the spot. Keep practising for all you're worth.

# Cabbing it

A cab is any trick that is done backwards, or opposite to the way it's usually done. That's why it's important, for example, to be able to turn confidently in any direction.

## Cab 360

**STEP 1** ▶

Choose a level and very smooth surface for your first attempt at skating backwards. Stand with feet apart, knees bent and lower yourself into a sitting position. Roll backwards, pushing with the inside edges and allowing your skates to move outwards.

◀ **STEP 2**

Bring your skates together. The toes should be splayed, the heels almost touching. Don't lift your skates off the ground at any time.

## STEP 3

Keep one foot steady. If you
are better at right-handed
crossovers, then this should be
your left foot. Push the right
foot out quite hard with the toe
pointing slightly inwards. Keep
most of your weight on the left
foot to aid balance.

## ◀ STEP 4

Pull, don't lift, your right
foot in slowly, using the
front wheels of the
pushing foot.

## STEP 5 ▶

Repeat using the right foot as
the anchor and the left as the
pushing foot. Then try the
move, pushing with both feet.

Once you've perfected the
basic moves for the cab 360,
you'll be able to roll-up hills
and round corners, backwards!

# Street wise

## Taking the rough with the smooth

Not all roads, paths and streets are the same. Some are rough and pot-holed, some are cracked and uneven, and some – thankfully – are smooth and perfect for blading. The basic rules are the same for any surface: Keep your knees bent and legs extended wide with your weight forwards.

If you see a rough surface ahead, move one skate (preferably the one with the brake) into the lead, keeping your knees bent and arms outstretched at waist height. The extended wheelbase gives you more stability and allows you to safety brake, turn or slalom to avoid the obstacle, or to raise one skate over the obstacle.

## Going up ...

Do not practice this on a busy road or pavement.

**STEP 1** ▶
Glide toward the kerb with one skate leading. Your weight is on the trailing skate.

**STEP 2** ▶
Put the leading skate on the kerb and transfer your weight onto it. Lift the trailing skate onto the kerb and glide forward.

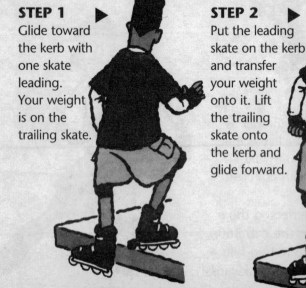

## ... Going down

The safest way is to come to a complete stop at the kerb and then step down side-ways. But if you don't want to lose too much speed, you can glide off the kerb as shown below. Four things to remember: Don't practice this on a busy road, check out what's coming, give yourself lots of time and check the surface you're about to glide onto.

**STEP 1**
Approach with the brake skate trailing. Check what's ahead and slow down. Keep your weight centred over both feet.

**STEP 2**
Glide, don't jump, off the kerb and bend your knees to absorb the impact. Extend an arm for balance.

## Head start

*If you've ice skated or snow skied you will take to in-line skating very quickly. The movement, the sense of balance and some of the moves of in-line skating first made their appearances on the rink or on the slope.*

# Making it to the top

If you can skate uphill successfully then you've got good skating technique down pat. For unless you can push with your inside edges, you'll never be able to skate up any sort of incline. Here are six hints for making it to the top:

1 Don't lean back on your heels.
2 Keep your weight centred over the balls of your feet.
3 Keep your knees bent.
4 Use your arms for balance.
5 Look where you're going and watch out for rough surfaces.
6 Keep to the left and don't pull out without looking behind t see if a skater, pedestrian, cyclist or car is coming alongside.

## Feel the burn

*Going up hills is a brilliant way to exercise leg muscles. It may be exhausting, but it's worth it for when you get to the summit you can cruise down. And don't worry, your helmet will prevent the rush of air messing up your hair. Safe and gorgeous at the same time!*

# Hills without spills

Okay, you can hare down a hill breaking all speed records, terrifying yourself and all who watch; or you can cruise down, stretching out the ride with big curves and turns. This mega-cool way of getting from summit to base camp is called traversing. It's the same technique that skiers and snowboarders use, so it can't be bad.

Before you launch yourself down a hill:
1 Look before you leap.
2 Stay in control by using slowing moves, a weaving slalom technique or by braking.
3 Check for nasty, wheel-snagging obstacles.

# Traversing

Traversing is all about controlling your speed
down a hill by turning across the slope.

### STEP 1

Head across the slope,
cutting a path that is
slightly downhill. The
uphill skate leads.

### ◀ STEP 2

Make the turns by rolling from
side-to-side on the corresponding
edges of your skates. Keep your arms
out in front for balance. Skates should
be parallel, but not too close together.
Bend your knees and point them
toward the slope. Put your weight
forward over your skates.

### STEP 3 ▶

Each time you traverse, push
the uphill skate into the leading
position before you take the
turn. The downhill leg will
support you through the turn.
If you pick up too much speed,
exist the turn slightly uphill.

### ◀ STEP 4

At the bottom of the slope, use the heel
brake to slow you down before skating
smoothly and safely on.

55

# The big quiz

*You're about halfway through this book, so it's time to check out how much you've taken in, how much you know about in-line culture and whether you've got what it takes to move onto the more difficult areas of aggressive, speed and hockey skating. Are you ready? Let's go.*

**1** Which of these celebs is not a known skater?
a) Tom Cruise, b) Liam Gallaher, c) Madonna.

**2** What are the main things to be when skating ?
a) polite, b) friendly, c) cool.

**3** What is a cab?
a) a New York taxi, b) a move done opposite to the usual way, c) a left-footed skater.

**4** Which of these is not a method of stopping?
a) T-stop, b) hockey stop, c) bus stop.

**5** How do aggressive skates differ from recreational skates? They ...
a) have no brake, b) are cooler, c) have smaller wheels.

**6** Which of these is a cool place to skate?
a) muddy path, b) busy street, c) seaside boardwalk.

**7** What is a spore (also known as a scrape)?
a) a plant, b) a stupid person with rental skates, c) a zit.

**8** What do you do if a dog is hot on your heels?
a) speed up to out-run it, b) hide, c) hit the brake.

**9** How many people in a roller hockey team?
a) five, b) three, c) ten.

**10** What are bearings?
a) things bears wear on their fingers, b) small balls inside the wheel, c) shock absorbers.

## WHAT'S YOUR SCORE?

| | |
|---|---|
| 1  a) 0, b) 2, c) 1 | 6  a) 0, b) 0, c) 2 |
| 2  a) 2, b) 2, c) 1 | 7  a) 0, b) 2, c) 0 |
| 3  a) 0, b) 2, c) 0 | 8  a) 1, b) 0, c) 2 |
| 4  a) 0, b) 0, c) 2 | 9  a) 2, b) 0, c) 0 |
| 5  a) 2, b) 0, c) 1 | 10  a) 0, b) 2, c) 0 |

**Between 15 and 20 points** – You know lots about in-line skating. You've got the right attitude, plus bags of common sense.

**Between 8 and 14 points** – You're well on your way, but just how good are you on the technical stuff?

**Between 0 and 7 points** – You could do with a few lessons in skating common sense. Go over all the moves again, this time with your thinking cap on.

# Keep on rolling on

One of the best things about in-line skating is that the gear is low maintenance. An occasional check of the brake, wheels and bearings will keep your skates rolling smoothly. But before and after a heavy session of massive airs, gruesome grinds and a couple of slams, a more thorough check-up should be carried out. And don't forget, if you know how your skates work then you'll know exactly what add-ons you'll need for your style of skating.

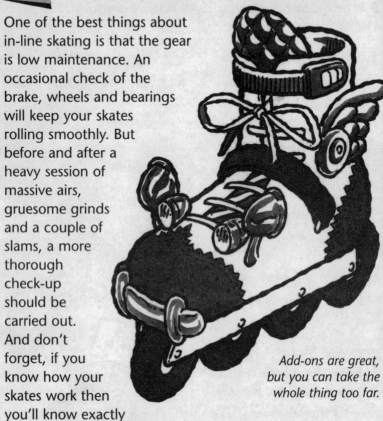

*Add-ons are great, but you can take the whole thing too far.*

## The size is right!

*Make sure you choose tools, spares and add-ons that fit your particular skates. Ask for advice at your local skate shop. Many skates come complete with the right tools.*

# The kit

BEARING GEL

It's a very good idea to put together a skate repair kit that you can keep in your skate bag, back-pack or bumbag. These are the basic bits and pieces you'll probably need: wrench, bearing removal tool (also called a three-way tool), screwdriver, cleaning rag, an old toothbrush, Allen key, bearing gel and cleaner, and spare bearings.

To keep youself in good repair, why not pack a tube of sunscreen cream, change for a telephone, a clean cloth, sticky plasters and a bottle of drinking water?

## Heel brake

Check your heel brake
occasionally to make sure
it hasn't worn down
excessively. When you first
start learning to skate you'll
use the brake a lot. As you
progress, you'll use
methods of stopping that
don't require slamming
down the brake. If the

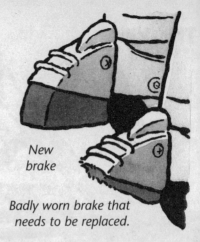

*New
brake*

*Badly worn brake that
needs to be replaced.*

brake needs to be replaced, don't worry – a new brake is
quite cheap to buy and installing it is very easy.

### Changing the heel brake

**1** Remove the rear wheel and axle.

**2** Remove the entire brake and surrounding bits.

**3** Use the correct screwdriver to unscrew the bolt.

**4** Pull the worn brake pad off, being careful not
to lose the nut in the brake support arm.

**5** Attach the new brake pad.

**6** Reattach the brake support to the frame and
replace the rear wheel.

### Rotating the wheels

Skating on hard or rough surfaces really wears down the
wheels, especially the inside edges. It's dangerous to ride on
worn wheels. On a turn, for example, the frame can scrape
along the ground causing the skate to slip and you to slam.

Slightly worn wheels don't need to be replaced. You can gain extra wheel-time by rotating them. Rotating involves swapping the position of each wheel so that worn edges are used less, and rounded edges are given a thrashing.

*New wheel*     *Worn wheel*

## Save the wheel

*Rotating the wheels will keep the edges rounded and even. They will last about four times longer than wheels that aren't rotated.*

Skaters work out a rotation sequence based on where the wheels have worn, but to simply even out wear, follow the diagram or simply move the front wheel to the back; then move each of the other wheels forward by one position. As you change the position of each wheel, turn it so that what was previously the inside edge becomes the outside edge.

### BUYING NEW WHEELS

When the time comes to buy new wheels, save some money by buying a set of four or eight. New wheel designs roll into the shops almost every day. Some are specially made for aggressive, hockey or speed skating, so get some advice before you buy.

## REMOVING AND REPLACING A WHEEL

◀ **STEP 1**
To remove a wheel: Hold the skate, boot-down, firmly between your knees and use the correct Allen key and wrench to loosen and unscrew the wheel bolt. It's best if you work on one wheel at a time. Remove the wheel bolt and lift out the wheel. Clean the wheel and turn it to even out wear, or change it for a new one.

**STEP 2** ▶
To replace the wheel: Drop the wheel into place and firmly tighten the wheel bolt with the Allen key and wrench. Spin the wheel to make sure that it's moving freely. As a final check, spin all the wheels to see if they spin for the same amount of time.

## WHEEL SIZE
Wheels for recreational skating range from 65mm to 82mm in diameter. You'll find the size marked on the side of the wheel. Basically, the larger the wheel the faster your skates will move. The biggest wheels are used by speed skaters, while smaller wheels are best suited for stunt, aggressive and dance (or freestyle) skates.

## WHEEL HARDNESS
The other mark that you'll see stamped on a wheel refers to how hard it is. The hardness is given a durometer rating

and it is indicated by the letter "A". Ratings range from about 70A to 100A. Normal wheels have a durometer rating of 78A. When deciding on a set of wheels, you may need to ask for advice about which hardness is the most appropriate for your style of skating.

Once you've made decisions about wheel size and hardness, you're left with choosing a colour. Wheels are made in every colour of the rainbow plus some, so be prepared for another long session in the skate shop!

## Bearings

Even the best-maintained bearings will wear out. In addition to general wear-and-tear, particles of sand, grit, rust and other foreign matter trapped inside the casing will further damage the bearings. If the bearings are making a strange noise, not spinning freely or not spinning at all, it's time to buy a new set.

When buying bearings, aim to get the best quality you can afford. Precision bearings, made by reputable manufacturers, give a smoother ride over a longer life.

### Watch out for the water

*Avoid skating through puddles, in the rain or in areas where there are damp leaves, grease or oil. Skating in these conditions is dangerous; it will also shorten the life of your bearings. If you skate through a puddle, continue skating on a dry surface for a while before hanging up your skates. This will help dry out the bearings.*

Bearings are rated by a special engineering grade number, ABEC. Bearings rated ABEC 1 or ABEC 3 are best for recreational skaters. Make sure that your bearings are rated at least ABEC 1.

*Outer bearing casing*          *Bearings*

## CHANGING AND CLEANING BEARINGS

### STEP 1 ▲

Remove the wheel (see page 62). Hold the wheel with the fingers of both hands and use the three-way tool to push the bearings casings out on both sides. After cleaning or replacing them, reposition the bearings using the three-way tool. Do not over tighten the bolt.

### STEP 2 ▲

To clean: use a soft cloth or toothbrush to clean the outer casing. The bearings should be cleaned with bearing cleaner and a cloth.

## Quick clean-up job

*Whenever you check your wheels, take a cloth and wipe off the grease and dirt that has accumulated on the bearings.*

# Rock and roll

If you think a rocker is someone who likes head-banging music and leather gear, you're wrong. Rocker refers to positioning the wheels so that they do not all rest on the ground at once. For example, on a four-wheel skate the centre two wheels can be lowered so that the front and back wheels are a couple of millimetres off the ground.

Setting your skates on a rocker allows you to turn and spin faster. Great news! The bad news is that rockered skates can be unstable at high speeds or over-long distances. Aggressive, hockey and dance skaters rocker their skates to give extra flexibility for extreme turns and tricks. Many aggressive skaters do what is called anti-rocker. This involves putting smaller diameter wheels in the centre two positions as an aid to grinding. And does it work? You bet!

The first time you rocker your skates, it'll feel really unstable and you'll be saying "No way, Jose." But give yourself time to get used to the effect and practise on a smooth surface (soft grass nearby is very reassuring) until you feel really confident.

## HOW TO ROCKER YOUR SKATES

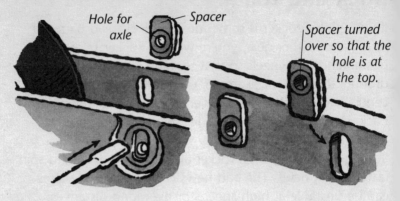

Hole for axle

Spacer

Spacer turned over so that the hole is at the top.

**STEP 1** ▲

When you remove the centre two wheels, you'll see oblong spacers inserted into holes in the frame. Each spacer has a hole through which the axle passes. Some spacers have two adjustment positions.

**STEP 2** ▲

Pop the spacers out and turn them over so the axle hole is towards the bottom of the frame. Reinstall the centre wheels and the axles.

# Grind plates

Aggressive skates take a real bashing from steps, rails and kerbs. To protect the frames, the skates are fitted with a piece of metal or heavy-duty plastic called a grind plate. When a grind plate has seen better days, it's replaced.

You can buy grind plates separately or as part of a "hop up" kit. These kits contain grind plates, bearings and all the tools you'll need.

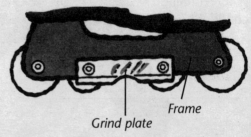

Frame

Grind plate

# What's hot, what's not

*If skating is overtaking your life, then you'd better make sure that you're doing it in the coolest way possible. Here are some hot dos and chilly don'ts.*

## What's hot

**1** Comfortable and practical gear.
**2** Being friendly to other skaters.
**3** Trying new moves because <u>you</u> want to.
**4** Being polite to other people using the park.
**5** Pizza.

## What's not

**1** Wearing expensive or branded, fashion-victim clothes.
**2** Thinking that skating makes you more attractive to the opposite sex.
**3** Attempting a move just to impress your mates.
**4** Buzzing people on the street and in the park.
**5** Burgers.

# 6 Getting aggressive

So you've been skating for a while, you've mastered the basics like skating backwards, crossovers and slaloms, and can even do a perfect T-stop. So what next? Are you really ready for the tough stuff? Are you ready for aggressive skating?

Aggressive skating is sometimes called extreme skating. This is the radical end of in-line skating, where things get seriously interesting. For a start, you can invent your own moves and tricks and enter competitions. Watching vert skating is dizzying. Riders almost fly, taking off into airs from special ramps and half-pipes. This type of skating may be exciting, but it's also extremely dangerous. It's not enough just to be confident and willing to have a go, you've got to be an ace skater. There are two types of aggressive skating – street and vert.

## STREET SKATING

When street skating you use whatever surfaces and obstacles you find in public places. Favoured sites are pavements, stairs, benches, walls and stair railings. Like vert, it involves performing tricks. Street skating isn't like a regular sport with lots of rules and disciplines, it's a way of life where skaters continually search for the ultimate ride.

## VERT SKATING

Vert (from the word vertical) skating has its roots in skateboarding. Vert, like much of skateboarding, is about doing mind-boggling tricks on ramps.

## Aggressive not aggro!

*Aggressive skating doesn't mean that you have to be aggressive people. Most skaters are laid-back types looking for fun. Be polite to other skaters or people in the park. They have just as much right to be there as you. If you're considerate you'll be able to use the park again and you won't ruin things for other skaters. If you're rude and appear to be damaging property, you'll be on your bike for good!*

# Are you ready?

*You shouldn't contemplate using a half-pipe or any kind of extreme skating ramp until you can perform these three moves. Makes sense, doesn't it, that should learn to walk before you run?*

## 1 GLIDING OFF KERBS

*You should be able to skate off a kerb forwards or backwards with complete confidence. Always keep your legs bent and use them as shock absorbers. Remember to approach the kerb with the non-braked skate leading. A glide off a kerb doesn't mean a jump into the yonder, it means moving like a swan on a pond – smoothly.*

## 2. SKATING BACKWARDS

*You've got to be able to skate backwards doing things like backwards crossover turns and transitions. (You can go over crossover turns on page 45.)*

*A transition will get you into a backwards-facing position and this is how you do it. Extend your right arm and foot backwards, and your left arm and foot forwards. Lift up your heels and pivot on the front wheels with your toes going with the turn. Arms and head shouldn't move. Lower your heels and you're ready to skate backwards.*

## 3. JUMPING

*Conquer the basics of jumping on the next page, then go onto the harder stuff. Learn jumping in easy stages, and when it comes to hitting the ramp for the first time, ask two mates to hold your arms to help you balance.*

# Jump to it

Before you leap tall buildings in a single bound, get used to jumping with two big skates attached to your feet. Start out by jumping over imaginary obstacles and then move onto jumping over a plank of wood mounted on bricks.

◄ **STEP 1**
Glide up to the jump, one foot will be in the lead. Near the jump, bend your knees and lean forward from the waist. Pull your arms back.

**STEP 2** ▶
Push down hard on the front of your skates. At the same time, uncoil and straighten your body and pull your arms forward. Don't look down – keep your head up and face the direction you're moving.

71

**STEP 3** ▶

Before landing, bend your knees and extend your arms out in front for balance. Land ready to glide with one foot slightly in front of the other.

# Skate ramp ahead!

Always use a proper skate ramp and remove your heel brake so that it can't snag on the ramp.

**STEP 1**

Skate fast towards the ramp. When you're about three metres away, move into a glide stance. Extend your arms, bend your knees and keep your body position low.

**STEP 2**

Glide onto the ramp at speed. Just before you reach the top of the ramp, give yourself an extra push. This will give your jump more height and length.

**STEP 3**

Tuck your knees up towards your chest. (Being able to tuck-up tight is necessary once you get into grabs.) Use your arms for balance.

**STEP 4**

As you lose height, move your feet into the landing position with one foot slightly in front of the other. Always keep your knees bent when landing to absorb the impact.

# Grinding into action

Grinding has nothing to do with coffee or making annoying noises with you teeth, but everything to do with making magic on wheels. A grind is when the skater jumps onto the edge of a railing (a stair rail or similar), kerb or bench and the skates slide along the edge.

Like lots of stuff in aggressive skating, grinding takes practice to perfect. Even top skaters spend days getting their grinds just right and along the way they hit the deck more than few times. Other than lots of protective padding and a good helmet, you'll also need the balancing skills of a high-wire artist, the stamina of a long-distance runner and the courage of a stunt actor. Are you up to it?

## Ground rules

Start grinding on something low like a kerb or low rail in a skate park, don't hit street iron just yet. If an area nearby provides a soft landing, then go for it. The most important thing to remember is to land on the rail or edge in precisely the position you want to complete your grind. Always know your limits, and only jump onto a rail if you know you can land safely.

If you haven't got grind plates on your skates, get some and fit them NOW! Grind plates will stop the chassis wearing down and help to give a smooth ride.

## Pro talk

*"There's definitely an adrenaline rush when you're doing big tricks. Grinding really long rails is the biggest buzz ever!"*
Charlie Cuthbertson, aggressive pro skater

# Fine grinds

There are four grinds that you should learn – the frontside, backside, royale and soul grind. These four moves are the basis for loads of other grinds like the topside soul, nearside soul, rock n'roll, smith grind, indy grind, shifty and unity.

# Frontside grind

**What is it?** A grind with your legs apart. Your back faces the rail or edge.

**How to do it:**
Make a speedy approach, almost parallel to the rail or edge. Make the jump so that you land with legs apart and with the rail or edge sliding between the centre wheels. Centre your weight between your legs and over the rail. Keep your knees bent. Position your arms as shown – outstretched and slightly forward of your body to help you balance. Hold this position throughout the grind.

**The exit:** When you get to the end of the rail or edge, jump and turn away from the rail in the direction you want to land.

# Backside grind

**What is it?** This is a variation of the frontside and uses the same riding technique. The only difference is that you face the rail or edge.

**How to do it:** Approach the rail or edge as you would for a frontside, but do a half-turn in the air as you jump up to the rail. Land facing the rail or edge with the rail or edge sliding between the centre wheels. Ride out the rail as you would for a frontside grind.

**The exit:** Jumping off is a bit more difficult as you can't see where you're going to land.

## Break pads

*Doing tricks like these could be really dangerous if you fall off. Always pad up when you're learning new moves.*

# Royale grind

**What is it:** Similar to the frontside grind except that your weight is on your back foot. You face in the direction that you're going on the rail. The back leg is bent and takes most of the body weight.

**How to do it:** As you approach the rail, you should be almost parallel with it. Land with your feet apart in a wide stance with the rail or kerb between the centre wheels. Balance over your back foot and keep your back leg bent. Keep a low centre of gravity. Throughout the grind the knees are bent and arms are out in front.

**The exit:** At the end of the rail, jump off in the direction you want to land.

# Soul grind

**What is it?** A frontside variation where you grind on the outside sole of the trailing skate.

◀ **STEP 1**
Approach the rail, kerb or bench (start out low, of course) from an angle with a reasonable amount of speed.

**STEP 2** ▶
Jump up and land with both feet on the rail or edge. The back foot is tilted forwards so that the knee is over the top of the rail. The wheels of the leading skate face forward. Most of your weight should be on your back skate; only a little on the leading skate. Look along the edge you're grinding and lean back.

◄ **STEP 3**
To come off the edge, twist your hips to help you straighten up. Look in the direction you're going.

## Watch and learn

The best way to learn tricks is to watch the good skaters. It's not enough just to ogle at their skill, concentrate and analyse each part of the move. In a grind, like the acid soul (right), you'd study the approach, how to land, body posture, which part of the skates (boot or frame) is grinding and how to exit.

*Acid soul grind*

## Slippery slide

*If the surface you are grinding is dead smooth and quite slippery you may not need to lean back so far.*

# Mixing it together

Once you've mastered the four basic grinds, you can customise them by throwing in extra moves. The torque soul, for example, is a basic soul grind but with the front foot boned over.

*Backside fahrvegnugen – great grind, but how do you say it?*

You can make up your own tricks by varying the approach (you can do it forwards or backwards), by introducing some airtime (spinning into and out of a trick) and with add-on variations (for example, topsides, farsides, overs, negatives, backsides, frontsides or switches).

Here are some suggestions for approaching a grind and for gaining some airtime cred.

**True spin:** Forward spinning used in the approach.
**Fakie spin:** Backward spinning for the approach or when riding away from the trick.
**Out spin or blind spin:** Fakie spinning in excess of a quarter of a revolution. Used in the approach to a move.
**Alley-oop:** Doing a trick in the opposite way to how you normally do it. In an alley-oop soul grind, the trailing foot becomes the leading foot.
**Zero spin:** A fakie air or jump with no spin in it.
**In spin:** Backward spinning for more than a quarter of a revolution into a trick.

## Know the lingo

*New words and tricks are being invented every day in aggressive skating. This isn't a sport that stands stills – if you snooze, you lose. Catch up on the lingo by checking out the Glossary on pages 119-120 and keep up with the latest by reading in-line skater magazines.*

# Stair riding

If you can grind a kerb and keep your balance, you're ready for stair riding forwards. (Yep, some do it backwards!)

Not all stairs are the same. You'd be crazy to ride steep, narrow stairs. Shallow, but wide stairs are the way to go. Never take on more than four steps when you first attempt stair riding.

**STEP 1**
As you approach the stairs, lean forwards slightly. Keep a stance that's as extended as possible so that both skates do not drop at the same time.

**STEP 2**
Let the front skate drop first, then the back skate. Land on the rear wheel of both skates.

**STEP 3**
Keep knees and ankles bent so that they absorb the shocks. Hang lose, don't tense up.

# Zero spin farside soul

This move sounds very complicated, but it isn't. The first part of the name tells you that there's no spin on dismount (phew!) and the rest tells you that this is a basic, everyday sort of grind manoeuvre ... well, almost.

◀ **STEP 1**
Approach the rail or kerb (practise on a low rail or kerb, please) backwards.

**STEP 2** ▶
Near the rail, bend your knees and jump onto the rail. Make it a big jump so that you start grinding far down the rail. Now you know why it's called farside!

◀ **STEP 3**

Ride the rail on the outside edge of the chassis of the leading foot (the downhill foot) as shown. The rail is grinding between the centre wheels of the trailing foot. Keep your arms out for balance and centre of gravity low.

**STEP 4** ▶

As you approach the end of the rail, prepare to dismount by bending your knees even further. Drop off the end of the rail. Don't get lazy and simply slip and slide off it.

◀ **STEP 5**

Drop to the ground without spinning, turn and skate away as cool as a cucumber!

81

# Vert-i-go-go

Vert skating is really a buzz, the big swing. The term vert comes from vertical and this should give you a good idea about what the main idea is – it's riding a vert ramp (also called a half-pipe) and doing tricks at the top.

## Finding your way around a vert ramp

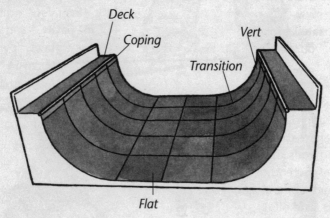

Deck

Coping

Vert

Transition

Flat

**Flat:** The centre floor of the ramp.
**Transition or trannie:** Curved sections of the ramp between the flat and the vert.
**Vert:** The steepest part of the ramp where the real action happens and how!
**Coping:** The metal railing at the top of vert that is used for grinds and other tricks like handstands.
**Deck:** Flat platform where skaters bail out or rest up.

When you first start vert skating you'd be wise to use a mini-ramp. Even though a mini-ramp is only half the size of a normal ramp (some competition ramps are even bigger) you can still get up enough speed to do airs. Half a vert ramp is called a quarter-pipe.

# Making the transition

Before you can get into the fancy stuff on the vert or on the coping, you've got to be able to make clean turns on the trannie.

**STEP 1** ▶

Approach the trannie at the angle, keeping low with legs apart. The leading skate is pointing in the direction you want to turn.

◀ **STEP 2**

With hands out in front and knees bent, carve a broad turn across the trannie. Stay low on the trannie – you'll have plenty of opportunities to scare yourself at the top.

**STEP 3** ▶

Turn back down the trannie towards the flat. Use your arms for the balance. Keep criss-crossing the trannie until you can turn confidently in both directions, then start to build up speed and height.

As you get higher and closer to the vert, you'll feel yourself almost come to a halt. It feels as if you're hanging in the air, suspended at the top of the turn. Just before this, you can make small jumps to complete the turn.

## Go low to go high

*To get higher up the ramp, bend at the knees and waist – almost in a crouched position – before you approach the trannie. As you enter it, release your body and explode into the ride. Incredible!*

# Catching some air

Any time you put some distance between yourself and the ground, you're doing an air. You can catch some air jumping out of a grind or off a skate ramp. But for big airs you need a vert ramp or quarter-pipe. Remember – the higher you go, the harder you fall.

*Parallel grab*

## Pro talk

*"If I had to describe aggressive skating in a five words, I'd say it's fun, fun, fun, fun, fun!"*
Charlie Cuthbertson, aggressive pro skater

# Making a grab

Holding a skate with one or both hands as part of a jump is a grab. You can also do a grab while you're in a spin.

There are lots of different sorts of grabs. A mute, for example, is bringing one arm across your body and over your legs and grabbing the skate. To do this successfully, your legs have to be tucked up and pushed close together. Angle your legs out to create a mute with a bit of style.

A Japan or judo is another sort of grab, but one that definitely takes practice. As you jump, kick one leg out in front (just like a judo kick) and bring the corresponding arm over your body to grab the skate on the other leg.

*Grinding the coping – the most fun you can have with skates on!*

# Can you cope?

Street style meets vert ramp when you grind the coping along the top of the vert.

To ride the coping, keep your knees slightly bent and your arms out in front for balance. Keep your legs wide apart, one well in front of the other, for maximum control.

# Pump it up

Here are some difficult moves that you may want to try once you've mastered the basics.

### HAND PLANT
A one- or two-armed handstand performed on the coping or deck after cutting up the vert.

### STALEFISH GRAB
One for the vert where you put one arm between your legs and grab the heel of a skate.

### SPINS
Once you've got some air, you can start to spin. A 180 spin is half a revolution, a 360 is a full revolution. To do big spins, like a 540, misty flip or corkscrew, you need a lot of air.

# Out with old, in with the new

Vert skating is always changing with new tricks pushing aside old ones every year. For many years, grab tricks were the business, but now spins and airs are what make the crowds cheer, hoot and whistle. And why not? Some pro skaters are spinning through 540 or 720 degrees (that's $1^1/2$ to 2 revolutions) at the top of the vert.

The parallel 540 is a neat but difficult trick. Let's face it, if you can't spin 180 then what chance have got at a 540? But for those of you who literally want to touch the sky, here's the ins and outs and the ups and downs of the parallel 540.

# Parallel 540

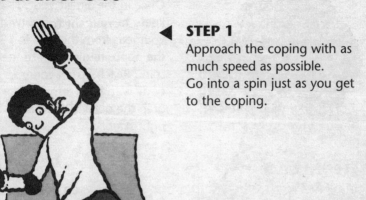

◀ **STEP 1**
Approach the coping with as much speed as possible.
Go into a spin just as you get to the coping.

**STEP 2**
Float, don't jump, off the vert using your head and shoulders to make you turn. Try to get lots of height as this will give you max time in which to perform the trick.

▶

## Parallel 540 tip

*When you're in the air, lift your knees up and twist your legs from your hips in the opposite direction to the way you're spinning.*

◄ **STEP 3**

Once in the air, lift your knees to your chest and twist your legs from the hips in the opposite direction to the spin. Reach across your body with both arms and grab the outside of your right skate.

**STEP 4** ▶

Keep the spin going by turning your head in the direction of the spin and looking over your shoulder. Your body will follow your head.

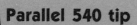

## Parallel 540 tip

*Look over your shoulder while you're spinning. It'll help to keep your spin going and going and going ...*

### STEP 5
Hold the grab for as long as possible. When you're ready to release, twist your legs and feet into a landing position. Look over your shoulder to see the ramp coming closer.

### STEP 6
Commit to your landing by stamping down firmly on the vert with your feet. Your body should be horizontal to the vert.

## Parallel 540 tip

*When your skates hit the vert, don't lean too far forward or back, you'll fall!*

# **Pucker up!**

If you've never played roller hockey, you don't know what you've been missing. As a game it's fast, exciting and great fun; as a boost to your social life, there are few other sports to beat it!

## Game on ice

*In-line hockey came about in the 1980s when ice hockey players in Northern America and Canada were looking for a way to train when ice-rinks were out of action and lakes had thawed.*

# Rules rule

The rules of hockey are based on ice hockey, with some differences to make it safer for the players. Here they are:

**1** All players should wear full protective gear – helmet; shin, knee and elbow pads; and padded shorts and gloves.

**2** The maximum number allowed on the pitch at one time is five players per team – four outfielders (two defenders and two wings/forwards) and one goalkeeper. While only five players are allowed on the pitch during play, a system of rolling-subs, chosen from the full team of 16, ensures that each player is substituted every two to three minutes.

**3** The international standard game is 60 minutes and is controlled by two referees. The duration of an average game is 44 minutes, and consists of two 20-minute halves with a four-minute break. A "drop in" game with your friends played in a park or on school grounds has no time restrictions. Players simply drop-in to the game whenever someone drops outs.

**4** A goal is scored when the whole of the ball passes completely over the front edge of the goal line between the vertical posts and under the cross-bar of the goal. It won't count if it's kicked or thrown into goal. Don't hit the ball or puck into your own goal – the goal will be awarded to your opponents.

## Fast in every way

*In-line hockey is the world's fastest-growing team sport. In the USA, in-line gear out sells ice hockey ten to one!*

# The gear

As a beginner skater all you need is a helmet, stick and puck. If you're just practising on your own you will not need pads. As soon as you start playing with friends and decide you really like the sport, then you will need to consider buying some protective gear, such as knee and wrist guards. If you are already a skater, you will probably have the necessary protective gear.

Remember, don't rush out and buy the serious gear until you're sure that you really like the sport. Beginners can improvise when it comes to safety gear. You can use a cycle helmet and skating pads or football and field hockey pads to start. As soon as the game becomes competitive you MUST invest in specialised equipment. As for the stick and puck, a field hockey stick and a tennis ball will do just fine.

## Cheesed off

*One of the great goalies of a championship in-line skating team started his career using a cheeseboard with a glove strapped to it and wore cricket pads for protection.*

## Getting serious

The price of equipment really varies, so watch out that you don't spend too much. Again, don't be bamboozled by sales people into thinking that you'll need all kinds of gadgets and accessories. The basics are a stick, a helmet, pads and a ball or puck. You can add the rest when you get better and have a bit more money to spend.

### SKATES

Use your normal recreational skates when you're starting out. If you end up playing to a high standard, you should buy a pair of hockey skates. To get the skates that will guarantee the sort of performance you'll need, be prepared to hand over quite a lot of money. So it's your choice, a pair of good hockey skates or 10 new CDs.

### PADDING

For the full suit of armour (elbow pads, shin pads and padded gloves and shorts) you'd better brace your parents for a wee shock. But if you're serious about the game, then it's only right that you're serious about safety. If you play for a school or league team, they may be able to buy bulk and pass the savings onto you.

### HELMET

If you're under 18 and playing in a league, you'll need a helmet with a face-cage.

## For boys only

*To protect those sensitive bits, buy a box. A good quality one costs about the same as one CD. Well worth it!*

### PUCK OR BALL
The official puck or ball should be made of plastic and there are strict guidelines about its size and weight.

### STICK
You can spend as little or as much as you like on a hockey stick. The official stick for league or international matches, should be made of wood or of an approved material; the butt end must be padded.

The maximum length of the stick from heel to the end of the shaft should be 147 centimetres, and 32 centimetres from the heel to the end of the blade.

The goalkeeper's stick should have a blade with a maximum width of nine centimetres and a minimum width of five centimetres.

If all this gear seems a bit pricy, remember that you only need the basics to get started. You could even get second-hand gear by putting a notice in a local magazine. Quality equipment will last you for a long time, so you can kit yourself out gradually.

## Where to play

You can play in-line hockey wherever you can find a smooth surface. Because car parks are not the safest (and you may well be thrown out), ask at your school or leisure centre if you can use an outdoor court.

The size of your playing area is largely determined by the number of players. If you're playing a "drop-in" game" you'll be able to judge for yourself how much space is needed to accommodate you and your friends. If you are playing a more serious game, you'll need an area 40 metres by 20 metres. The official goal cage dimensions are 1.85 metres wide by 1.20 metres high.

Use anything you can find to mark out the perimeter of your playing area and the goal posts in an informal game. It won't be the first time that a motley collection of sweatshirts, back-packs and plastic containers will have been used. If you're lucky to be able to use an empty car park, don't push your luck by using the shopping trolleys.

## Skills U Need

You have to be able to skate to a reasonable level and be confident with hockey stops, skating backwards and doing tight turns in both directions. But another invaluable skill to being an ace in-line hockey player is having played field hockey. Some of the pros actually think that being able to play hockey is more important that being able to skate.

Once you're in the game, learn to play with your head up. In other words, no looking down at your skates while you race around the pitch. This is especially important when dribbling the ball. Don't look at the ball or puck until you're ready to pass.

If you're new to hockey, practice your stick handling so you get used to the feeling of the ball or puck being in contact with the blade of the stick. Go out and have a knock-around game with your mates. Concentrate on mastering passing, receiving and dribbling the ball.

# How to handle the stick

**1** The stance – legs shoulder width apart and knees bent over your toes. Your shoulders should be in line with your knees and toes, and your head should be up.

**2** Grip the top of the stick with one hand and place the other hand about 45 centimetres down the stick.

**3** When you move the stick from side to side, let your wrists, not your body, roll. Transfer your weight from leg to leg.

**4** When the stick comes in contact with the ball or puck, contact should be smooth. Lift the blade over the ball to receive it.

**5** To prevent bouncing, slightly cup the top of the blade over the ball or puck.

### Give it some stick

Using the stick, make small strokes to tap the ball or puck from left to right. When you first try you'll find it really hard not to look down. You'll soon get used to the vibration that the ball or puck hitting the blade creates and looking down just won't be necessary. Next step is to make the strokes wider so that the ball or puck is really travelling.

# Passing and receiving drills

Make two teams of five people with each team forming a circle. Pass the ball or puck around and across the circle. See which team can make the most passes in 40 seconds.

For the next drill, each player has a ball or puck. The idea is to keep the balls or pucks moving from player to player in one direction around the circle.

# Hand-eye co-ordination

Flick a ball up into the air with the blade and bounce it off the blade as many times as you can. How good are you? If you can bounce it three times, you're doing well; five times is terrific; and 10 times – very cool!

# Give it a shot

Now it's time to work on some shots. Speed and accuracy in getting the shot away are key factors in goal scoring. For accuracy, the ball or puck should come off the middle of the blade.

## Wrist shot

Called a surprise shot because if done well it will surprise everyone!

Twist your upper body to transfer your weight to the stick and onto the skate nearest the ball or puck. With a tight grip on the stick, bring your arms forward and snap your wrists forward at the same time to send the ball or puck on its way.

## Forehand sweep shot

This is one of the more accurate shots as the ball or puck is in contact with the blade throughout the sweeping motion.

Spread your hands wide on the stick and bring the ball or puck to the side of your body, just behind your back skate. Lean forward, transferring your weight onto your front skate. Bring the ball or puck forward with the blade. For a low shot, tilt the blade over the ball; for a high shot, tilt the blade under the ball. As the blade reaches your front skate, tighten your grip, extend your arms and rotate your body. At that instant, snap your wrists to propel the ball or puck away.

## Slap shot

The slap shot can be developed once you have mastered the wrist shot. Use it to make distance shots at great speed.

*Slap shot – a classic hockey shot on foot or wheels.*

## Snap shot

Similar to the wrist shot, but the blade of the stick is pulled back from the ball or puck just before the shot is taken. The blade is never raised higher than the hip in the back swing.

98

## Flip shot

The flip shot is used to lift the ball or puck up so that it clears the defensive zone, a fallen goalkeeper, or to shoot it in to the offensive end.

This is how it's done: bend the knee closest to the ball or puck, and scoop up the ball or puck off the floor with the blade of your stick. Shoot the ball or puck away. The follow through with the stick should be high.

## Can do, can't do

*You **can** touch, with your hand, a ball or puck that is in the air so as to guide it to your stick.*

*You **can** raise your stick above your head as long as it's not dangerous to an opponent or official.*

*You **cannot** attempt to play a ball that is above shoulder height with any part of your stick.*

# How to receive a pass

1 Keep two hands on the stick and your elbows away from your body.

2 The blade of your stick must be touching the ground and angled square to the incoming pass.

3 Try to keep your hands and arms relaxed so that they absorb the shock of the received pass. Twisting your wrists slightly will tilt the blade and further cushion the impact of a ball or puck that's really moving.

4 Keep your eye on the ball or puck whenever waiting for a pass.

## Foul Play — In-line hockey commandments

**1** A player must not charge – charging is taking two steps at a run towards an opponent.

**2** There shall also be no tripping, holding, hooking, kicking or any other such violent nonsense, thank you very much.

**3** A player must not cross-check – pushing a player with the shaft of the stick while the stick's off the ground and held in both hands. Sometimes accidental, but always illegal.

**4** A player must not slide-tackle – in other words, no feet-first contact with an opponent

**5** A player must not poke, spear or take a swing at an opponent (and definitely not the ref) with the stick.

And if you do – you'll be penalised by being sent to the sin bin to cool off. If you're a multiple offender, you'll be sent off! How embarrassing!

# Positions, please

This is how you should be lined-up for the start of the game. If you're still like this five minutes into the first half, something has gone terribly wrong.

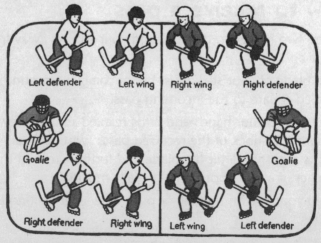

Left defender   Left wing   Right wing   Right defender

Goalie                                    Goalie

Right defender   Right wing   Left wing   Left defender

## DEFENCE

Good defence is vital to a winning team. A dominant defence requires lots of discipline and skill to break up attacking plays and prevent goal-scoring shots. As a defender you have to stop the other team getting the puck, and if they do get it you have to get it back.

The golden rule of defence is: Let the puck or the player go past you, but never let both go past at the same time!

## WING/FORWARD

Main job is to hassle (only in legal ways, of course) the other team's defence. Hassle your own defence and you'll be in trouble. While trying to win the puck, the wing also tries to shake the marking opposition player.

## GOALKEEPER

The goalkeeper protects the goal and he or she can stop the ball with any part of their body or stick as long the ball is within the goal area or on the goal line. Once outside the goal, the goalie follows the same rules as the other players.

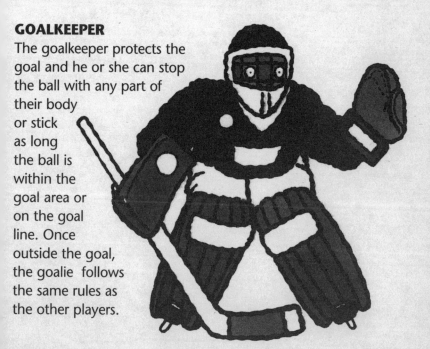

# Clubbing together!

If you want to get really competitive you could set up your own team and challenge other teams to matches. You can get in contact with other teams by trawling local parks, in-line skate shops and by putting up signs on the noticeboards at skate parks, leisure centres, post offices, newsagents and at school.

Skater magazines (see page 117) often include contact addresses for in-line organisations and for special events. If there's a league match or big comp on somewhere, you're bound to come across like-minded bods who are desperate to join a team.

# 8 The need for speed

## The dream ...

Picture this. You're skating a marathon with 30 other skaters in a tight pack doing about 40 kilometres an hour. The wind is whistling by your head, your legs are moving in a perfect rhythmic stride, the road ahead is mesmerising, as you match the other skaters stride for stride.

Suddenly you pull out all the stops and surge ahead. You find yourself leading the pack with only metres between you and the finish line.

Can you do it? Have you got what it takes to win?

From somewhere deep inside, you find the energy to make a few more power strokes. Your nearest competitors fall further behind. You cross the line. You're the winner!

There's no doubt about it. In-line racing has a very high adrenaline buzz. There is the thrill from winning a race, as well as the exhilaration of having challenged yourself and won through.

# The sport

Speed skating is probably one of the fastest-growing areas of in-line skating with people from five to 75 testing their endurance and skating skills in races of up to 160 kilometres (100 miles) long. There are different lengths of races from sprints to marathons. You need to be properly trained and 100 percent fit.

# The stance

Once you've got the hang of stroking and gliding, you can take it a stage further and have a go at advanced or in-line striding. This is the movement used by speed skaters and advanced in-liners.

## Wheely fast

*The 10-kilometre (6.2 mile) race is the most popular distance for in-line racing. There have been 10-kilometre races held all over the world, sometimes with more than 1,000 competitors in each race. The fastest skaters finish the course in less than 15 minutes, racing at an amazing 38.6 kilometres (24.8 miles) per hour.*

If you look at speed skaters in a race you will see that they keep their body position very low with the knee of the gliding leg bent almost at a right angle. Their back is flat in order to hold this position and their heads are up and always looking in the direction they're moving. They swing their arms in huge arcs across their body in perfect time with their strides to help them pick up speed. When they are cruising at speed they often keep their arms behind their backs.

This crouched stance helps prevent wind drag so that the racer is as aerodynamic as possible.

## The gear

Speed skaters wear tight one-piece suits or shorts and tops made of Lycra. This very smooth fabric is completely body-hugging and makes the skaters as streamlined as possible. They always wear wrist guards and helmets because falling at speeds in excess of 80 kilometres (50 miles) per hour is very dangerous. Seriously competitive speed skaters don't wear knee or elbow pads as they create unwanted drag.

Most speed skaters wear skates with five wheels instead of four. You can use recreational skates for speed skating, but for a smoother, faster ride replace the existing wheels with harder and larger diameter wheels.

# On your marks ...

The start of a race can be a pretty scary place. All the skaters are bunched up together, each trying to get the best start. Skaters need to get away very quickly and get into their stride as soon as possible.

Speed skaters pace themselves. Just like long-distance runners they have worked out where their skills are best used. They may start quickly with the leaders and then drop back, conserve some energy, and then speed up for the finish. Other skaters maintain a regular speed throughout the race; a pace that will get them to the finishing line first. If you try long-distance or sprint skating, you need to work out what racing technique is best for you. Most sprints are just that – an out-and-out hard and fast race over a very short distance.

## Slipstreaming away

Just like cyclists in the Tour de France race, one of the easiest places to ride is in the slipstream of the leaders. The slipstream will be found just behind the leading pack. Here a skater will come across little or no drag resistance from the wind, but will also benefit from a sort of "sucking" effect that will increase their speed.

## Resting up

*Always rest well between races or sprints to give your muscles a chance to relax. The chances of being injured increases many times if you are tired or unwell. Don't give racing a thought if you're injured.*

## And the winner is . . .

As the race nears its end, the main pack of skaters gradually accelerate. With the finish line in sight, the leading skaters will try to break away and sprint to the line. They each try to hold back this sprint for as long as possible so as to conserve energy and to avoid giving another racer any sort of advantage. Races are won and lost in these closing and always exciting moments.

# Want to hang out with a fast crowd?

If you're interested in taking up speed skating, it's important that you join a club in order to develop the best training programme and to learn the skills and tactics. Speed skating is a very athletic sport, you will need to build strength and endurance by doing regular exercise and eating properly.

# So you want to be a pro?

Anyone who's ever skated has dreamed of winning big competitions and becoming a professional skater. Being professional means having a massive sponsorship deal (in other words, you are paid to skate) and getting the latest gear from your sponsors for free. You have to, of course, be seen to use the sponsor's equipment in competitions and exhibitions.

It seems like skate heaven, but the reality is a little different. As any professional will tell you, being a pro skater is hard work. You have to be able to perform at your peak all the time – there's no down-time for injury or bad hair days – winning competitions and dazzling the crowds at exhibitions with new tricks and feats-on-wheels. There's also massive amounts of time spent travelling. Yep, being a pro is a great life, but it requires commitment.

wow!

## So you want to be a pro?

Most of the top skaters are sponsored by the mega-big manufacturers of skates and gear, for example, Rollerblade, Oxygen, Heavy and Fila. But in addition there are the manufacturers of wheels, bearings and pads that also sponsor many of the big-name skaters.

Basically, it works by the sponsor providing the skater with money in order to pay for his travel and other expenses whilst competing in tournaments and championships. In return, the skater wears their products, and promotes and represents the brand in advertising and in public appearances.

## Look at me!

To find a sponsor you need to get yourself seen out and about. You'll need to hang out and session the big skate parks and take part in as many smaller championships as you can. Manufacturers send out scouts to these events to spot the hottest talent.

So you want to be a pro?

## Pro talk

*"Our sponsors change all the time. We can be sponsored by two or three manufacturers at one time depending on who's out there."*

Jeremy Bolton, member of the Hyper Street Cruisers, European Skaterhockey champions.

## Getting sponsored

If you think you've got what it takes to turn pro, you could contact your local skate shop and ask if they will sponsor you. There may also be a small, local business, say a clothes or sports shop, that could benefit from being associated with a talented skater who loves mixing it with the kids at the skate park and who is willing to put in a good word for the business. If you've got a hockey team, why not ask the sponsorship deal-makers from one of the equipment companies to come down and watch your team play.

Do a bit of self-promotion by sending photos of yourself doing knock-out tricks or competing to a skate mag or to a local paper. Anything you can do to raise your profile increases your chances of being picked up by sponsor.

## Lights, camera, action!

*Chris Edwards is one of the most famous pro vert skaters in the world. He's appeared in adverts for breakfast cereals and drink companies, as well being a movie stunt-double.*

# Want to know more?

Each branch of in-line has a different organisation looking after its interests. If you need advice or want more information you could write to the organisations below:

**Skate: The British In-Line Skating Association (BISA)**
Tel: 01869 345953

**International In-Line Skating Association (IISA)**
Address: 201 N. Front St.
306, Wilmington, NC
28401 USA
Tel: 910 762 7004

**National In-Line Hockey Association**
Address: 999 Brickell Avenue, 9th Floor, Miami,
FL 33131 USA.

**USA Hockey In-Line**
Address: 4965 N, 30th Street, Colorado Springs,
CO 80919 USA.

**Aggressive Skaters Association**
Address: 171 Pier Aven, STe247, Santa Monica, California,
90405 USA.
Web address: Skating The Infobahn

# Skate parks and shops

This is a small selection of parks and shops that you can try contacting in your local area. This list will give you a starting point if you're trying to track down other parks or or need to get hold of hard-to-find equipment. Telephone numbers have been supplied whenever possible.

## Skate parks

### UNITED KINGDOM

Birmingham: Wheels Adventure Park (0121) 771 0725
Birmingham: Vertical Extreme (0121) 635 1025
Bristol: Rollermania (0117) 927 9981
Bristol: Skate and Ride (0117) 907 9995
Bury St Edmunds: Rollerbury (01284) 701216
Derby: Rollerworld (01332) 345828
Derby: Storm Skate Park (01332) 201768
Herne Bay: Pier Pavilion (01227) 366921
Hornchurch: Romford Skate Park (01708) 474429
Ipswich: Rollerking (01473) 611333
London: The Playstation (020) 8969 4669
Norwich: Superskate (01603) 403220
Stockport: Skate USA (0161) 483 1898

### AUSTRALIA

Brisbane: Petrie Terrace, across from Lang Park
Canberra: Belconnen

**Want to know more?**

Melbourne: Westerfolds Park, Beaconsfield Parade
Melbourne: St Kilda Fast Trip
Melbourne: Jells Park
Melbourne: Hawthorn Velodrome
Sydney: Moore Park

**SOUTH AFRICA**
Capetown: Prichard Security Skatepark
Johannesburg: Boogaloos Skatepark (001) 622 6185
Johannesburg: Look Ahead Skatepark (001) 793 6613
Krugersdorp: Legends Skatepark
Natal: Aston Bay Ramp
Natal: Rox Skatepark (031) 561 2442
Natal: Surf News Skateboard Park
Pretoria: Pink Pipe Skatepark (012) 549 3009
Pretoria East: Skateboard Warehouse Skateboard

# Skate Shops

**UNITED KINGDOM**
Cardiff: Pro Line Skates (029) 2023 7360
Cardiff: Skateside (029) 2055 5311
Devon: Brookite Blades (01837) 53315
Devon: Apex Sport Skate World (01803) 663346
Kent: Skate World (0181) 303 3761
Lancashire: Flying Skates (01257) 793529
Lancashire: The Grind (01253) 789379
London: Road Runner (020) 7792 0584
London: Blade and Skate Centre (020) 7581 2039
London: Blue Room (020) 7495 5444
London: Skaters Paradise (020) 8532 8530
Middlesex: Skate Aggressive (020) 8570 9904
Newcastle: NSC Northern Skate Centre (0191) 230 2595
Oxford: SS20 Skate Shop (01865) 791851

Portsmouth: Skaters Paradise (01705) 295 360
Surrey: Mayfair Skates (020) 8394 1987

## IRELAND

Marathon Sports are possibly the biggest retailers of in-line gear in Ireland. Contact Marathon Sports head office in Grafton Street, Dublin for details of branch stores.

## AUSTRALIA

Brisbane, Qld: Skate Biz (07) 3220 0157
Cronulla, NSW: Sheridan's (02) 9523 5675
Claremont WA: Bladeskate (09) 9246 9200
Fremantle, WA: Momentum Skate Shop (09) 9430 4082
Melbourne, Vic: PSC (03) 9783 3811
Homebush, NSW: Room 101 (02) 9763 1555
Surry Hills, NSW: Shut up and Skate (02) 9360 3113

## SOUTH AFRICA

Durban: Board Sailing
  (031) 337 4069
East London: Billabong
  (0423) 931 210
Johannesburg: Boogaloos
  (011) 823 4312
Port Elizabeth: Beach Break
  (041) 554 303

**Want to know more?**

# Cyberskate

Check out these internet sites for information about skating. There's loads of new sites appearing every week and lots that are regularly updated, so use your search engine to seek out **skate, skating** or **in-line** and see what you can come up with. Good surfing!

Road Runner
**www.roadrunner.co.uk**
Loads of the latest information about the Road Runner skate shop and the Playstation skate park. Packed with action footage, photo galleries and a virtual reality movie of the skate park.

**beserk.distribution@virgin.net**

In-line Skating Association
**www.iisa.org/**

SkateGRRL
**www.skategrrl.com**

**Skating.com**
The skater's online magazine

Heavy Urethane America
**www.heavy.com**

# Read all about it!

## Magazines

In-line skating magazines are a brilliant way of keeping
up with what's hot in the ever-changing world of in-line
skating. They'll give you the low-down on the latest
equipment and the inside track on new skate parks. There
are letters to read, real-life stories, interview with pros,
competitions and guides to doing new moves. They're also
jammed with fab photographs and funky ads.

You'll find some of the magazines on the shelves of larger
newsagencies and in skate shops. Some skate shops even
sell hard-to-get overseas magazines. Here's a selection for
the mag rack:

### In-Line Skater

All forms of skating are covered in this magazine. It has a
useful advice section and lots of tips for beginners. Back
copies are available if you need to check out how to do a
particular move.
Address: 13645 Beta Road, Dallas, Texas 75244 USA.

### Box

Aggressive skating mag with real-life stories of skating
crazies from all over the world.
Address: PO Box 15398, North Hollywood, California
91615-9714 USA

## Want to know more?

### Fourinarow
Aggressive skating magazine from Australia with lots of great shots and equipment reviews.
Address: 386A Clarendon Street, South Melbourne, Victoria, Australia
email: fourrow@mail.austasia.net

### Daily Bread
The bible of aggressive skating.
Address: PO Box 1026, Escondido, California, 92033-1026 USA

### Ist In-line
Covers all aspects of in-line skating, reviews of gear, interviews and step-by-step guides to all the great moves.
Address: The Mark Fitzpatrick Building, 188 York Way, London N7 9QR

For an aggressive skating overload or for massive gear reviews, look out for **Unity** or **Beserk**.

# Glossary

The names of tricks can be very confusing in in-line skating. Nobody seems to agree on what things should be called. Many definitions in this list have been sourced from *Daily Bread* magazine.

**Adrenaline**      Feeling of a rush of excitement

**Airtime**      Spinning in the air or jumping

**Alley-oop**      Forward spinning more than 90 degrees into the trick

**Approach**      How you skate into a trick

**Backside grind**      Grinding or sliding down a rail with your back facing the rail

**Chassis**      Base of the skate where wheels, brake and grind plate are found. Also called the frame

**Coping**      Railings at the top of the vert ramp

**Crossovers**      Where feet crossover in a turn

**Exit**      How you finish or come out of a trick

**Fluid**      Smooth or flowing move

**Frontside**      Aggressive skating move where skaters jump onto rails with legs apart

**Glide**      Gaining momentum by returning the stroke leg to a position under your body

**Grind**      Sliding over surfaces on the chassis of the skate

**Grind plates**      Metal plates that fit onto the frame of aggressive skates

**Half-pipe**      U-shaped ramp

**Hop up kits**      Special kits to accessorise your skates

**In spin**      Fakie spinning more than 90 degrees on the exit

**Integrated brake**      Brake that's included on your skate

**Jack**      To hit yourself on something while skating

# Glossary

| | |
|---|---|
| **Japan** | A vert jump where you grab the opposite foot with one hand |
| **Lid** | Helmet |
| **Mute** | Grabbing your boot in a jump |
| **Out spin** | Fakie spinning more than 90 degrees on the exit of a trick |
| **Pads** | Protective gear |
| **Parallel 540** | High jump off the vert ramp with a 540 degree spin |
| **Planters** | Grabbing your boot in a jump |
| **Pros** | Professional, as in pro skaters |
| **Pail** | Hand-rail on stairs that's used for grinding |
| **Revert** | Spinning off the rail in the same direction than you spun on |
| **Rewind** | Spinning off the rail in the opposite direction to the way you spun on |
| **Road rash** | Skate term for cuts and grazes from falling over |
| **Riding** | As in "stair-riding" down steps |
| **Royale** | Same as the frontside grind in aggressive skating, but shifting your balance backwards |
| **Scrape** | Stupid person on rental equipment |
| **Session** | Performing moves and tricks on a ramp |
| **Slalom** | Weaving movement |
| **Slammed** | Falling over when skating |
| **Spore** | Novice skater or one on rented skates |
| **Street iron** | Stair rails found in public places for grinding |
| **Stroke** | Outward movement of your leg that moves you forward when skating |
| **True spin** | Forward spinning more than 90 degrees away from a trick |
| **Variation** | Taking a trick and then changing it |
| **Vert** | U-shaped ramp. Also, a section of competitions held on a vert ramp |
| **Wind draught** | The place behind other skaters who form a wind-break in speed skating |
| **Zero spin** | Fakie with no spin |

# Index

# Index

## super.activ

# All you need to know

| | | | |
|---|---|---|---|
| 0 340 773294 | Acting | £3.99 | ☐ |
| 0 340 764686 | Athletics | £3.99 | ☐ |
| 0 340 791578 | Basketball | £3.99 | ☐ |
| 0 340 791535 | Cartooning | £3.99 | ☐ |
| 0 340 791624 | Chess | £3.99 | ☐ |
| 0 340 791586 | Computers Unlimited | £3.99 | ☐ |
| 0 340 79156X | Cricket | £3.99 | ☐ |
| 0 340 791594 | Drawing | £3.99 | ☐ |
| 0 340 791632 | Film-making | £3.99 | ☐ |
| 0 340 791675 | Fishing | £3.99 | ☐ |
| 0 340 791519 | Football | £3.99 | ☐ |
| 0 340 76466X | Golf | £3.99 | ☐ |
| 0 340 778970 | Gymnastics | £3.99 | ☐ |
| 0 340 791527 | In-line Skating | £3.99 | ☐ |
| 0 340 749504 | Karate | £3.99 | ☐ |
| 0 340 791640 | The Internet | £3.99 | ☐ |
| 0 340 791683 | Memory Workout | £3.99 | ☐ |
| 0 340 736283 | Pop Music | £3.99 | ☐ |
| 0 340 791551 | Riding | £3.99 | ☐ |
| 0 340 791659 | Rugby | £3.99 | ☐ |
| 0 340 791608 | Skateboarding | £3.99 | ☐ |
| 0 340 791667 | Snowboarding | £3.99 | ☐ |
| 0 340 791616 | Swimming | £3.99 | ☐ |
| 0 340 764465 | Tennis | £3.99 | ☐ |
| 0 340 773332 | Writing | £3.99 | ☐ |
| 0 340 791543 | Your Own Website | £3.99 | ☐ |

Turn the page to find out how to order these books.

# ORDER FORM

Books in the super.activ series are available at your local bookshop, or can be ordered direct from the publisher. A complete list of titles is given on the previous page. Just tick the titles you would like and complete the details below. Prices and availability are subject to change without prior notice.

Please enclose a cheque or postal order made payable to Bookpoint Ltd, and send to: Hodder Children's Books, Cash Sales Dept, Bookpoint, 39 Milton Park, Abingdon, Oxon OX14 4TD. Email address: orders@bookpoint.co.uk.

If you would prefer to pay by credit card, our call centre team would be delighted to take your order by telephone. Our direct line is 01235 400414 (lines open 9.00 am – 6.00 pm, Monday to Saturday; 24-hour message answering service). Alternatively you can send a fax on 01235 400454.

Title ......... First name ....................... Surname ...................................

Address .............................................................................................

...........................................................................................................

...........................................................................................................

Daytime tel ..................................... Postcode.....................................

If you would prefer to post a credit card order, please complete the following.

Please debit my Visa/Access/Diner's Card/American Express (delete as applicable) card number:

| | | | | | | | | | | | | | | | | |
|---|---|---|---|---|---|---|---|---|---|---|---|---|---|---|---|---|

Signature ........................................................Expiry Date ...................

If you would NOT like to receive further information on our products, please tick ☐ .